Fishing

Written by Sandra Iversen • Illustrated by Stephanie Walker

In the summertime,
Mom likes to go fishing.

She takes her fishing line,
her hooks, her bait,
and her hat.

Mom puts some bait
on her hook.
She throws her line
into the water and she waits.

She waits and she waits
and she waits.
At last, she feels the fish bite.
She pulls in her line.
No fish and no bait.

Mom puts some more bait on her hook.
She throws her line
into the water and she waits.
At last, she feels
the fish bite again.

She pulls on her line.
She pulls in a little crab.
"A little crab!" says Mom.
"We can't eat a little crab
for dinner!"
She throws the little crab
back into the water.

Mom puts some more bait on her hook.
She throws her line
into the water.
Then she waits and she waits
and she waits.
At last, she feels a big fish bite.

Mom pulls on her line.
She pulls and she pulls
and she pulls.
She pulls harder and harder
and harder.

“A boot!” says Mom.
“No more fishing!”